W9-DHR-867

IS THERE LIFE ON OTHER PLANETS?

by Isaac Asimov

DELL YEARLING · NONFICTION

Published by
Dell Publishing
a division of
Bantam Doubleday Dell Publishing Group, Inc.
666 Fifth Avenue
New York, New York 10103

The reproduction rights to all photographs and illustrations in this book are controlled by the individuals or institutions credited on page 32 and may not be reproduced without their permission.

Consultant: Fran Millhouser

Text copyright © 1989 by Nightfall, Inc.
End matter copyright © 1989 by Gareth Stevens, Inc.
Format copyright © 1989 by Gareth Stevens, Inc.

All rights reserved. No part of this book may be reproduced or transmitted in any form or by any means, electronic or mechanical, including photocopying, recording, or by any information storage and retrieval system, without the written permission of the Publisher, except where permitted by law. For information address Gareth Stevens, Inc., RiverCenter Building, Suite 201, 1555 North RiverCenter Drive, Milwaukee, Wisconsin 53212.

The trademark Yearling® is registered in the U.S. Patent and Trademark Office.
The trademark Dell® is registered in the U.S. Patent and Trademark Office.

ISBN: 0-440-40348-0

Reprinted by arrangement with Gareth Stevens, Inc.

Printed in the United States of America
September 1990

10 9 8 7 6 5 4 3 2 1

CONTENTS

Nowadays, we have seen planets up close, all the way to distant Neptune. We have mapped Venus through its clouds. We have seen the rings around Neptune and the ice volcanoes on Triton, one of Neptune's moons. We have detected strange objects no one knew anything about until recently: quasars, pulsars, black holes. We have learned amazing facts about how the Universe was born and have some ideas about how it may die. Nothing can be more astonishing and more interesting.

Yet one thing we have not discovered in the Universe is life. Oh, there is life on Earth, of course, but is that a very miraculous accident so that we are alone in the Universe? Or has life developed on some other world — perhaps on many worlds? That is something that interests scientists very much, and everybody else, too. So in this book, we will talk about life on other planets.

Isaac Asimov

The Basics — Life on Earth

Over three billion years ago, life appeared on the young Earth in the form of tiny bacteria-like cells. These cells were built up of common types of atoms: carbon, hydrogen, oxygen, nitrogen, and sulfur.

At first, these atoms made up very simple combinations with each other. But sunlight contains energy, and this energy forced the atoms into more complicated combinations, until small cells formed.

On any planet just like Earth, with the same chemicals and temperature, scientists think that life would probably form in the same way. But we don't know how many such planets there might be.

Single-celled bacteria are among the simplest forms of life known. Some bacteria help us digest our food. Some can make us sick. And some, like the bacterium shown above, live in damp sponges and swim across your kitchen table.

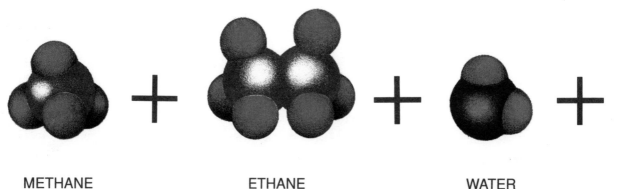

METHANE + ETHANE + WATER +

A formula for a "building block" of life. When these chemical ingredients are circulated in water and exposed to energy in the form of sunlight or ultraviolet light, they form glycine, one of the "building blocks" that help form life.

The young Earth's deep basins fill with water, forming our planet's vast oceans. Large meteorites still crash into the surface. These are the conditions under which life developed on Earth.

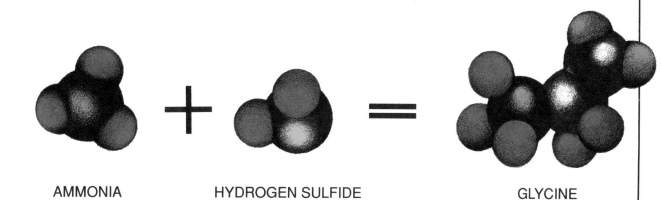

AMMONIA + HYDROGEN SULFIDE = GLYCINE

Above: A spark in a mixture of gases common in Earth's early atmosphere forms a brown tar of complex molecules.

Left: a diagram of a simple life experiment. Experiments first performed in the 1950s showed how simple gases (upper left square of diagram) and electrical sparks (upper right square) could form the complex molecules needed for life on Earth.

Making the Leap — Intelligent Life

For more than a billion years, life on Earth continued to consist of nothing more than simple cells. Gradually, more complicated cells developed, and these cells eventually combined with each other to form larger organisms. The more complicated an organism, the larger its brain and the more intelligent it might be.

It was only a few million years ago that the ancestors of human beings began the process of developing our kind of mind and our kind of thinking. So even though it may be easy for life to develop, it is not so easy for intelligence to develop.

A slice through the history of life on Earth. Important events are noted.

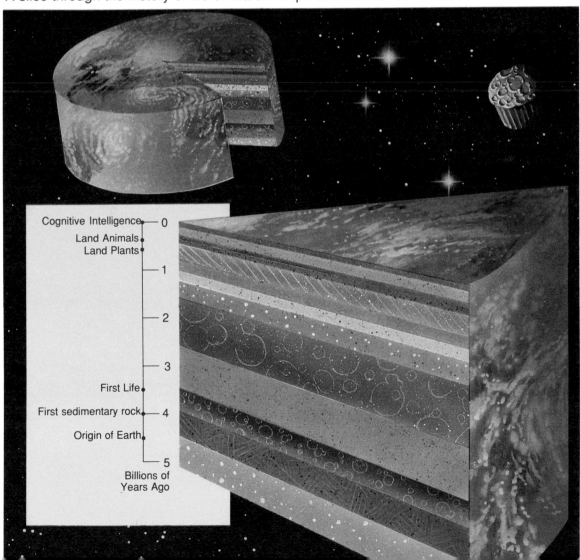

Cognitive Intelligence — 0
Land Animals
Land Plants
— 1
— 2
— 3
First Life
First sedimentary rock — 4
Origin of Earth
— 5
Billions of
Years Ago

Searching the Skies

We now know that the other planets of our Solar system do not have intelligent life. But what if intelligent life forms existed on planets in distant solar systems? How would we discover that such life forms exist? We can't go there, and perhaps they can't come here. Still, they might send out messages in the form of radio waves streaking across space.

It would take time, though. Messages from the nearest star would take 4.3 years to reach us. Messages from the other side of the Galaxy would take about 70,000 years. And of course, we might not understand the messages when we got them. But scientists are trying to detect such messages. Their work is called "Search for Extraterrestrial Intelligence," or "SETI."

A message from Earth, beamed from a radio telescope in 1974. When properly decoded, it describes our Solar system (▪▪▪▪▪▪), the radio telescope that sent the message (⋀⋔), and what we look like (🛉).

An artist imagines the distant future. Far beyond the cozy confines of our Solar system, dolphinlike life forms make contact with the Voyager probe.

Voyagers 1 and 2 carried a record of music and human voices, and pictures of our planet. The record jacket explains how to play the record and tells where it came from.

Did life's building blocks invade Earth from space?

Where did the chemicals needed for life on Earth come from? For years, scientists have thought that energy — from sunlight or even lightning — probably caused atoms and molecules on prehistoric Earth to form these chemicals. Today, scientists have found many of these same chemicals in material from space, like meteoroids and comets. Did life on Earth begin when some of these bodies hit Earth — and brought the basic "building blocks" of life with them?

9

Wondering and Thinking

For hundreds of years, people have been interested in the possibility of life on other planets. In the 1600s, people discovered that the Moon and planets are worlds, just as Earth is a world. Naturally, everyone wondered if there might be life on those worlds, too.

As late as the 1830s, there were articles in a New York newspaper saying that life had been discovered on the Moon. Many people believed what they read, but the story was a hoax. There is no air or water on the Moon, and so there is no life.

In the 1870s, some astronomers saw straight lines on Mars and thought they were canals built by civilized beings. That was mistaken, too. There is very little air and water on Mars — not enough for complex life forms.

Below, right: Astronomer Percival Lowell made this globe of Mars in 1901. It shows straight lines once thought by some to be canals made by Martians.

Mars — once a living planet?

The Viking probes that landed on Mars found no life there, and all the water on it is frozen. Still, Mars has markings that look exactly like dry riverbeds. Is it possible that Mars was once warmer than it is now and had rivers or even seas? If so, life may have once developed upon it. Even now, there may be simple life forms on it that the probes have not detected. In the future, more probes — or even people — may go to Mars to settle this mystery.

Left: Believe it or not, this is what some people thought lunar inhabitants looked like.

Below: An artist's concept of what some people thought the Moon looked like. During the Great Moon Hoax of 1835, the New York *Sun* reported the discovery of all kinds of lunar life.

Extraterrestrial Life in Books and Magazines

In the 1920s and 1930s, magazines devoted to science fiction began to appear. Writers were looking for exciting and dramatic ideas, and they described our sister planets as filled with life. Usually, the life was described as monstrous and as threatening to conquer Earth. H. G. Wells had written a novel about a Martian invasion of Earth as far back as 1898, and many writers followed his example.

These were often very exciting stories, but there was no actual evidence that such life existed. Though there might well be life on planets that were like Earth, none of our neighbor planets was anything like Earth.

Venus — once Earth's twin?

Venus is almost the same size as Earth and is made up of the same kinds of rocks. It probably started off like Earth, with water oceans. Over time, however, it became a hot, lifeless wasteland. Venus is closer to the Sun than Earth is, but scientists don't think that is enough to explain the difference. We're not sure what happened to make Venus and Earth so different today. Perhaps if we knew, we could help prevent Earth from one day becoming like Venus.

Above: In *War of the Worlds*, H. G. Wells stirred fears of an invasion by terrible beings from Mars.

Opposite: Recognize these characters? Our picture of alien life is limited by our experiences on Earth. For instance, do you think aliens must have two arms and two legs?

Below: Venus might have started off a lot like Earth.

The Space Age — Setting the Record Straight

Until not so long ago, scientists could only study other worlds of the Solar system from a distance. Only from what they saw at these great distances could they reason that these worlds were too cold, too hot, too large, or too small for life to develop. But beginning in the early 1960s, scientists have been sending probes to take pictures of and study the conditions on other planets.

These probes have shown Venus to be boiling hot. They have also shown that Mars has no canals but seems instead to be mostly one large desert. Human beings have landed on the Moon, and probes have landed on Mars and Venus. For now, we have found no signs of even the simplest life, and we are certain there is no civilized life on these worlds.

Below: the surface of Mars as seen from the Viking lander.

Jupiter — life among the clouds?

Jupiter is almost all gas, mostly hydrogen and helium, with other substances present in small quantities, like ammonia, methane, water, and carbon. The outermost layers of Jupiter's huge atmosphere are very frigid. But as one sinks lower, the atmosphere rapidly warms to temperatures of thousands of degrees. Temperatures are comfortable at intermediate layers. Can life forms exist at this level of Jupiter's atmosphere? Some day, we might find out.

An African plant specially adapted to harsh desert conditions.

An artist's concept of Martian plant life.

Life in the Solar System? — The Facts As We Know Them

We know so much more about the Solar system now than just a few decades ago. We have mapped Venus right through its clouds, and we know that its surface is hot enough to melt lead. It has an atmosphere that is almost 90 times as thick as ours and almost all carbon dioxide. The clouds contain deadly sulfuric acid.

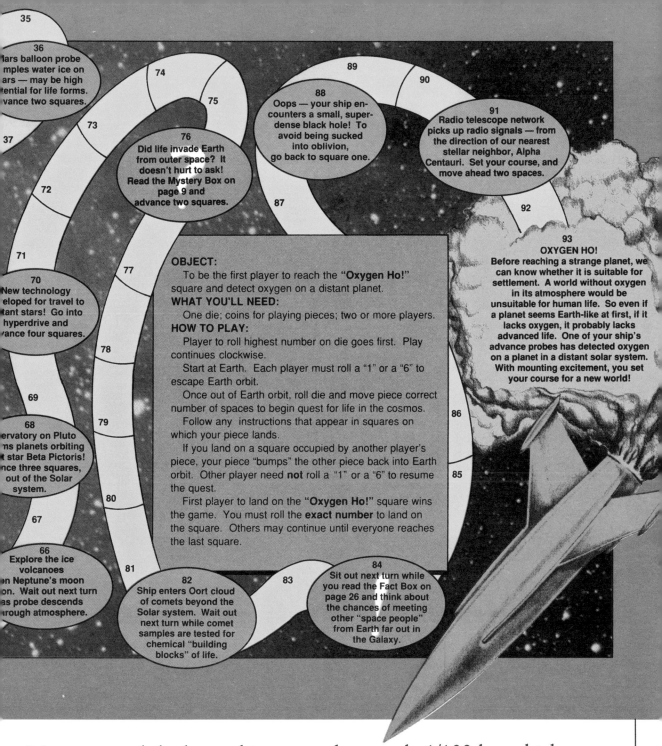

35

36
Mars balloon probe [sa]mples water ice on [M]ars — may be high [pot]ential for life forms. [Ad]vance two squares.

37

74

75

73

72

71

76
Did life invade Earth from outer space? It doesn't hurt to ask! Read the Mystery Box on page 9 and advance two squares.

89

90

88
Oops — your ship encounters a small, super-dense black hole! To avoid being sucked into oblivion, go back to square one.

91
Radio telescope network picks up radio signals — from the direction of our nearest stellar neighbor, Alpha Centauri. Set your course, and move ahead two spaces.

92

87

93
OXYGEN HO!
Before reaching a strange planet, we can know whether it is suitable for settlement. A world without oxygen in its atmosphere would be unsuitable for human life. So even if a planet seems Earth-like at first, if it lacks oxygen, it probably lacks advanced life. One of your ship's advance probes has detected oxygen on a planet in a distant solar system. With mounting excitement, you set your course for a new world!

70
[N]ew technology [dev]eloped for travel to [dist]ant stars! Go into [a] hyperdrive and [adv]ance four squares.

77

78

69

79

OBJECT:
To be the first player to reach the **"Oxygen Ho!"** square and detect oxygen on a distant planet.

WHAT YOU'LL NEED:
One die; coins for playing pieces; two or more players.

HOW TO PLAY:
Player to roll highest number on die goes first. Play continues clockwise.

Start at Earth. Each player must roll a "1" or a "6" to escape Earth orbit.

Once out of Earth orbit, roll die and move piece correct number of spaces to begin quest for life in the cosmos.

Follow any instructions that appear in squares on which your piece lands.

If you land on a square occupied by another player's piece, your piece "bumps" the other piece back into Earth orbit. Other player need **not** roll a "1" or a "6" to resume the quest.

First player to land on the **"Oxygen Ho!"** square wins the game. You must roll the **exact number** to land on the square. Others may continue until everyone reaches the last square.

86

85

68
[Obs]ervatory on Pluto [fin]ds planets orbiting [the] star Beta Pictoris! [Adva]nce three squares, [and] out of the Solar system.

80

67

66
Explore the ice volcanoes [o]n Neptune's moon [Trit]on. Wait out next turn [as] probe descends [th]rough atmosphere.

81

82
Ship enters Oort cloud of comets beyond the Solar system. Wait out next turn while comet samples are tested for chemical "building blocks" of life.

83

84
Sit out next turn while you read the Fact Box on page 26 and think about the chances of meeting other "space people" from Earth far out in the Galaxy.

Mars, meanwhile, has a thin atmosphere, only 1/100th as thick as ours, and its surface is often colder than Antarctica. Jupiter is just a huge ball of mainly hydrogen, helium, and other gases, and so are the other large planets. Their moons seem to be lumps of rock and ice.

These are the facts as we know them. And we know from these facts that Earth is the only known planet that can support life like ours.

Can We Still Hope?

Though the other worlds of the Solar system can't support life like ours, might they have other, strange forms of life?

One of Jupiter's satellites, Europa, is covered with a worldwide glacier. Perhaps under the ice there is a large ocean. Might there be life forms in it that are completely different from anything on Earth?

One of Saturn's satellites, Titan, has a thick atmosphere, and one of Neptune's satellites, Triton, has a thinner atmosphere. Under those atmospheres, there might be oceans of methane or ammonia. Could there be strange life there, too? Some day we might go to those worlds to find out.

An artist imagines life existing in an ocean under the icy surface of Europa, one of Jupiter's moons.

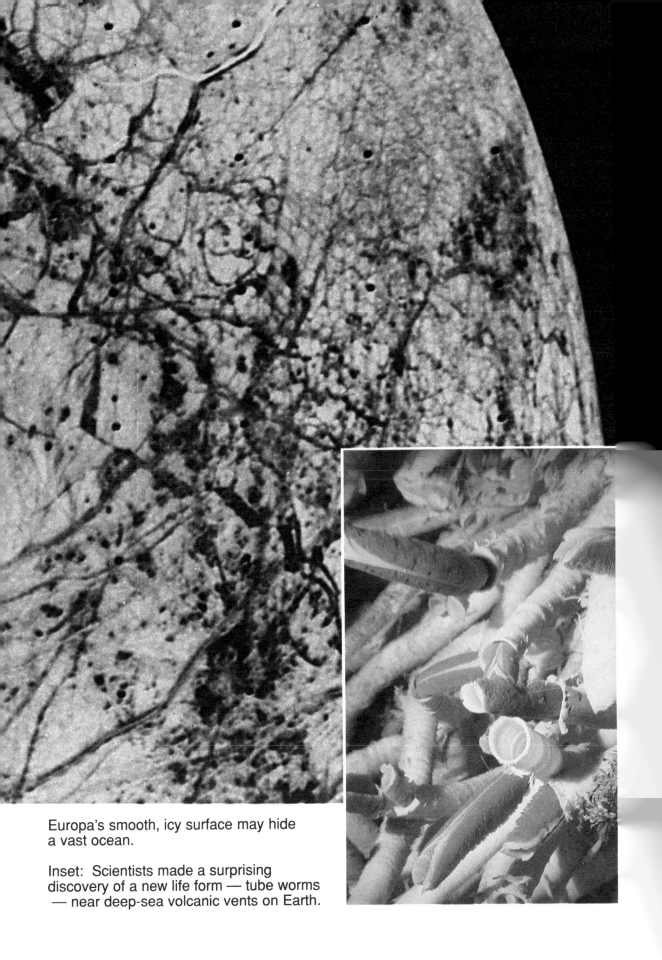

Europa's smooth, icy surface may hide
a vast ocean.

Inset: Scientists made a surprising
discovery of a new life form — tube worms
— near deep-sea volcanic vents on Earth.

The Universe Is a Big Place!

We know there is no life like ours anywhere in the Solar system beyond Earth. And for now, we can only guess about the chances of even simpler life beyond Earth. But even if there is no life in the Solar system, there are other stars in our Galaxy and beyond, and many of them must have planets circling them.

Our Galaxy has about 200 billion stars, and there may be as many as 100 billion other galaxies. Even if only <u>one percent</u> of the stars are like our Sun, and only <u>one percent</u> of those stars have planets like Earth, that would still mean billions of billions of Earth-like planets. Perhaps on every one of them there is life, and on a few of them civilizations may have developed. Some may even be advanced far beyond ours. We have no way of telling so far. We can only speculate.

Below: We live on one of nine known planets orbiting our Sun — one of 200 billion stars in the Milky Way (inset, opposite), which is but one of billions of other galaxies.

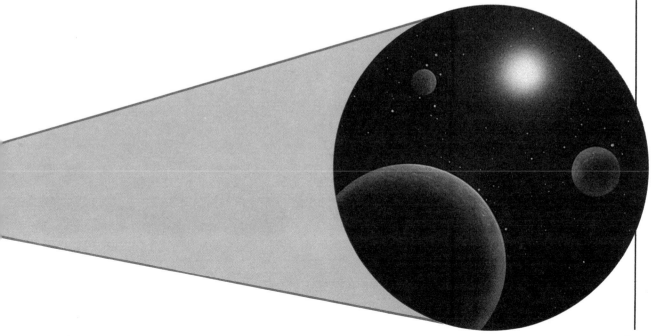

21

"What Would Life Be Like . . . ?"

Would life on some distant Earth-like planet seem familiar to us? Would there be creatures who look like human beings? Surely not! Even here on Earth, life takes a wide variety of shapes. Compare a whale and a crow; a praying mantis and a shark; a bacterium and an oak tree.

On other worlds, life would develop in strange ways to fit strange environments. Some might seem unpleasant to us, and some beautiful, but all of these possible life forms should be interesting.

Perhaps, in studying completely different life forms, we will understand all of life — and ourselves — better.

Looking for life in a harsh environment. Scientists are studying Antarctic lakes to get an idea about past environments on Mars.

Inset, opposite: The black, white, and green stripes are actually plant life called lichen (LIE-ken) growing in Antarctic sandstone.
Opposite: These rod-shaped bacteria grow along with the Antarctic lichen.

Below: Lake Hoare on the frozen continent of Antarctica.

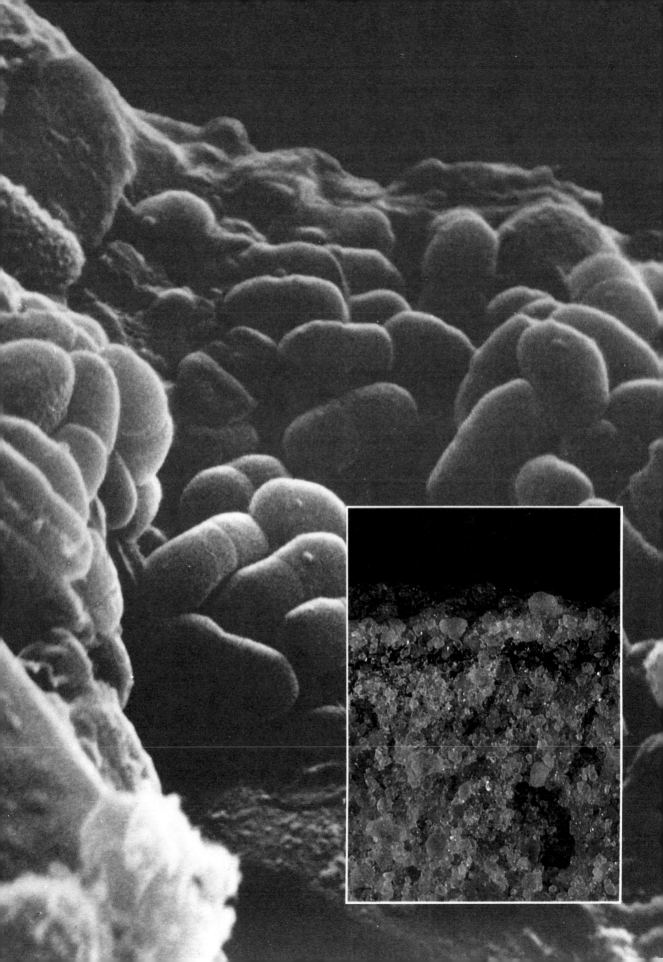

Are We Alone?

Suppose there is life on planets orbiting other stars. Can you imagine traveling to those planets to study those life forms? Rockets that take only a few days to reach the Moon, and a few months to reach Mars, would take many years to reach the stars.

Future rockets might travel 40,000 miles (64,000 km) each second, but they would still take more than 20 years to reach the nearest star. Even if you traveled at the speed of light (the fastest possible), it would take 100,000 years to go from one end of the Galaxy to another.

So even if there is advanced life out there among the stars, how will we reach it? Will we remain alone on our little planet?

A disk of dust and gas encircles the star Beta Pictoris. In the photo below, the disk is colored red and yellow; the star itself is masked out. Scientists believe the dust and gas are condensing into planets, forming a young solar system around the star.

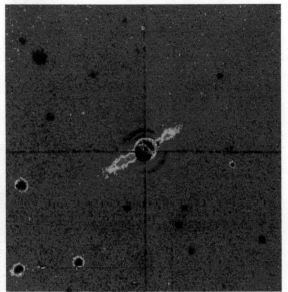

Inset, opposite: Farewell to Earth. An interstellar spaceship leaves Earth orbit and begins its long voyage to the stars.

Opposite: The starship from Earth surveys its new home — the planetary system of a remote star.

The Universe-wide Civilization

Reaching the stars is not something we can do in a few weeks, months, or even years. But suppose we take our time. Suppose we build huge starships that are small worlds in themselves with 100,000 people aboard each one, and that these ships travel through space on voyages that take thousands of years. One ship might eventually reach one distant planet, while others would reach other planets.

Slowly, humanity would settle among the stars and perhaps encounter other forms of life. Of course, it would be difficult for one settlement to communicate with another, and each would develop in isolation. Earth would become a distant memory, and some day it might be forgotten altogether.

Our descendants might become "extraterrestrials" to other interstellar civilizations. And should their paths ever cross in the vastness of the cosmos, our spacefaring settlers might even become extraterrestrials to each other!

After centuries of travel, an Earth ship and its inhabitants prepare for arrival at a new world.

The distant galaxies — plenty to go around

There is room in our Galaxy for millions of settlements, each near a different star. Beyond our Galaxy, there are others. There are three small galaxies, the Magellanic Clouds, some 150,000 light-years away. The nearest large galaxy, larger than our own, is the Andromeda Galaxy, which is 2,200,000 light-years away. The farthest known galaxies may be 17 billion light-years away. We will never use up the Universe or see all its glories up close.

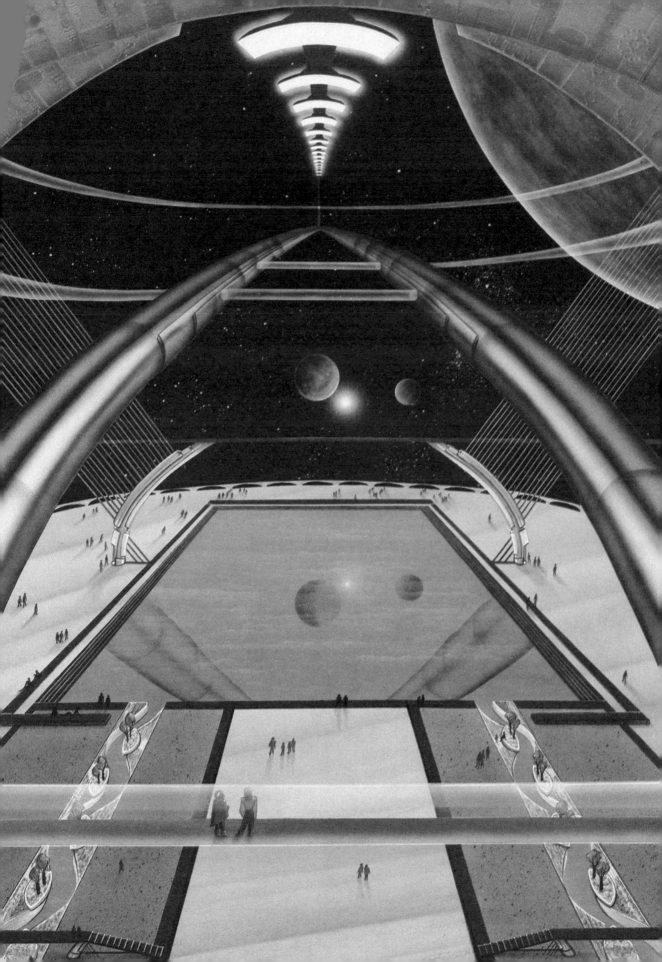

Fact File: Looking For Life in "Uninhabited" Places

So far, we haven't found any life on other planets. But does this mean that other planets are uninhabited? If we haven't found any life in a specific place, such as a distant planet or even a house down the street, we might call that place "uninhabited." But we might be amazed to discover how an "uninhabited" house actually teems with life forms — even if we don't see any of these life forms at first glance. Many of these forms seem alien to us, and they live under conditions that might seem hostile to life. The photographs and numbered chart on these two pages show just a few of these life forms.

Could it be that, like our "uninhabited" house, other planets harbor unusual life forms surviving under harsh conditions — and that we just haven't found them yet?

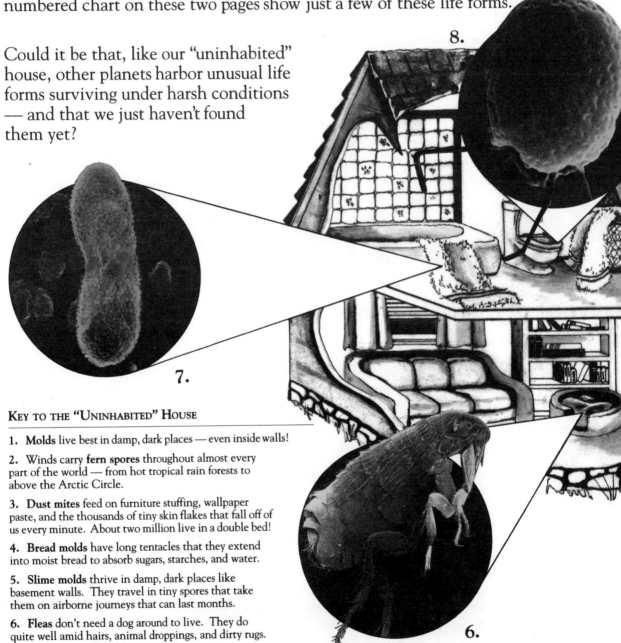

8.

7.

6.

KEY TO THE "UNINHABITED" HOUSE

1. **Molds** live best in damp, dark places — even inside walls!

2. Winds carry **fern spores** throughout almost every part of the world — from hot tropical rain forests to above the Arctic Circle.

3. **Dust mites** feed on furniture stuffing, wallpaper paste, and the thousands of tiny skin flakes that fall off of us every minute. About two million live in a double bed!

4. **Bread molds** have long tentacles that they extend into moist bread to absorb sugars, starches, and water.

5. **Slime molds** thrive in damp, dark places like basement walls. They travel in tiny spores that take them on airborne journeys that can last months.

6. **Fleas** don't need a dog around to live. They do quite well amid hairs, animal droppings, and dirty rugs.

7. Some life forms need surroundings that would kill other life forms, including humans. For example, this **bacterium** needs an environment <u>without</u> air!

8. Some **bacteria** exist in tough shells that protect them against hostile surroundings.

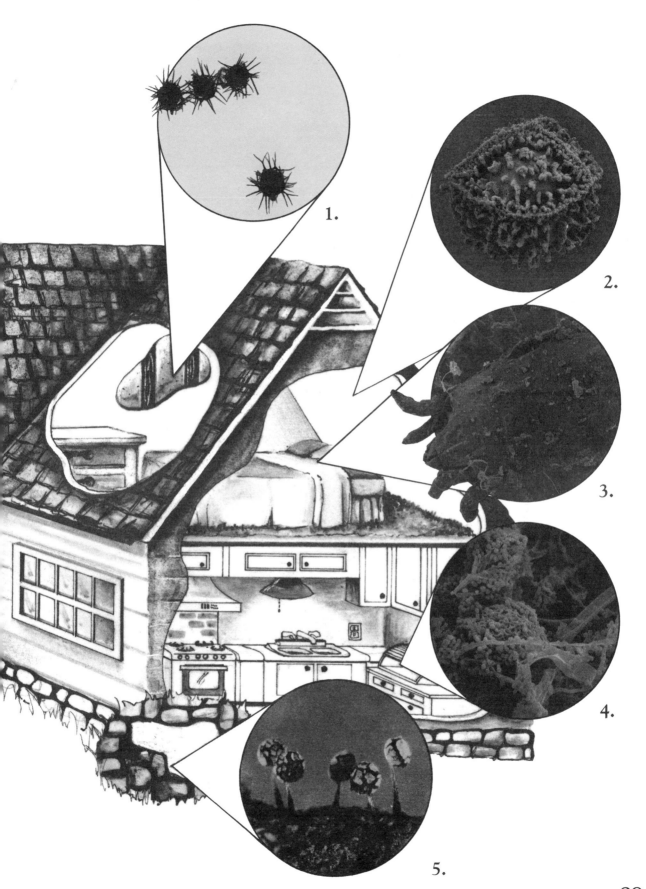

1.

2.

3.

4.

5.

More Books About Extraterrestrial Life

Here are more books about the possibilities of extraterrestrial life. If you are interested in them, check your library or bookstore.

Ancient Astronauts. Thorne (Crestwood)
The Case of the Ancient Astronauts. Gallagher (Raintree)
Cosmic Quest: Searching for Intelligent Life Among the Stars.
    Poynter and Klein (Macmillan)
Earth Invaded. Asimov (Raintree)
Is There Life on Other Planets? Woods and Woods (EMC)
Meet E. T. the Extra-Terrestrial. Klimo (Simon & Schuster)
Mysteries of Life Beyond Earth. Branley (Lodestar)
Other Worlds: Is There Life Out There? Darling (Dillon)
Science Fiction, Science Fact. Asimov (Gareth Stevens)
Strangers from the Stars. Etchemendy (Avon)
Unidentified Flying Objects. Asimov (Gareth Stevens)

Places to Visit

You can look into the chances of life among the other planets and stars without leaving Earth. Here are some museums and centers where you can find a variety of space exhibits.

Ontario Science Centre
Toronto, Ontario

Lawrence Hall of Science
Berkeley, California

Edmonton Space Sciences Centre
Edmonton, Alberta

National Museum of Science and Technology
Ottawa, Ontario

Hayden Planetarium-Museum of Science
Boston, Massachusetts

NASA John F. Kennedy Space Center
Kennedy Space Center, Florida

NASA Lewis Research Center
Cleveland, Ohio

Science World
Vancouver, British Columbia

For More Information About Extraterrestrial Life

Here are some places you can write to for more information about life in other parts of the Universe. Be sure to tell them exactly what you want to know about or see. Remember to include your age, full name, and address.

For information about planetary exploration and the search for extraterrestrial life:
The Planetary Society
65 North Catalina
Pasadena, California 91106

About unidentified flying objects:
J. Allen Hynek Center for UFO Studies
2457 W. Peterson
Chicago, Illinois 60659

About astronomy and planetary missions:
NASA Jet Propulsion Laboratory
Public Affairs 180-201
4800 Oak Grove Drive
Pasadena, California 91109

To report a UFO sighting:
UFO Reporting Center
24-hour telephone
(206) 722-3000

Glossary

atmosphere: the gases that surround a planet, star, or moon.

atoms: the smallest particles of elements that can exist.

bacteria: the smallest and simplest forms of cell life. A bacterium is one-celled and can live in soil, water, air, food, plants, and animals, including humans.

billion: in North America — and in this book — the number represented by 1 followed by nine zeroes — 1,000,000,000. In some places, such as the United Kingdom (Britain), this number is called "a thousand million." In these places, one billion would then be represented by 1 followed by *12* zeroes — 1,000,000,000,000: a million million, a number known in North America as a trillion.

black hole: a massive object — usually a collapsed star — so tightly packed that not even light can escape the force of its gravity.

canal: a river or waterway made by people to move water from one place to another. It was once thought that the narrow, dark markings on Mars were canals built by Martians to move water from the ice caps to the desert areas.

carbon dioxide: a heavy, colorless, odorless gas. Carbon dioxide gives soda its fizz, and is exhaled by humans and animals.

extraterrestrial: "outside of Earth." *Extraterrestrial* refers to forms of life that do not begin on Earth.

galaxy: any of the many large groupings of stars, gas, and dust that exist in the Universe.

glacier: an enormous layer of ice formed from compacted snow, often itself carrying a layer of snow.

hoax: an act that is intended to deceive.

host: a living organism on which or in which lives another organism, called a parasite.

hydrogen: the lightest gas in Earth's atmosphere. It is the most common gas in the atmospheres of the outermost planets of the Solar system.

interstellar: between or among the stars.

methane: an odorless, colorless, flammable gas. It is an important source of hydrogen. It was one of the gases present in the early atmosphere of Earth.

organism: anything that lives, such as a bacterium, a rose, a human — including any plant or animal.

oxygen: the gas in Earth's atmosphere that makes human and animal life possible. Simple life forms changed carbon dioxide to oxygen as life evolved on Earth. Oxygen makes up 1/5 of Earth's atmosphere.

probe: a craft that travels in space, photographing celestial bodies and even landing on some of them.

radio waves: electromagnetic waves that can be detected by radio receiving equipment.

satellite: a smaller body orbiting a larger body. The Moon is Earth's <u>natural</u> satellite. Sputnik 1 and Sputnik 2 were Earth's first <u>artificial</u> satellites.

science fiction: fiction, or stories, in which actual, imagined, and sometimes possible future discoveries in science form part of the story.

SETI: "Search for Extraterrestrial Intelligence"; the search for signs of extraterrestrial intelligence by trying to detect any radio signals that such intelligence might use.

spore: a single cell from which a new organism can grow.

sulfuric acid: a liquid that is capable of burning, wearing away, or dissolving many materials.

Index

The publishers wish to thank the following for permission to reproduce copyright material: front cover, p. 9 (upper), © Rick Sternbach; pp. 4 (upper), 4-5 (lower), 13 (upper), Matthew Groshek/© Gareth Stevens, Inc.; p. 5 (upper), © Dorothy Sigler Norton; p. 6 (upper), photograph courtesy of Dr. Bishun Khare/Cornell University; pp. 6 (lower), 7, © Garret Moore, 1988; p. 8, National Astronomy and Ionosphere Center/ Cornell University; pp. 9 (lower), 19 (large), 24, Jet Propulsion Laboratory; p. 10 (lower), photograph courtesy of Lowell Observatory; pp. 10 (upper), 11 (upper), © Lee Bataglia; p. 11 (lower), painting by Don Davis, courtesy of Sky Publishing Corporation; p. 12 (upper), The Museum of Modern Art Film Stills Archive; p. 12 (lower), Photofest; p. 13 (lower), © Alan Gutierrez; pp. 14-15 (lower), National Space Science Data Center; p. 15 (upper left), © Michael Carroll, 1988; p. 15 (upper right), Field Museum of Natural History, #B83024c; pp. 16-17, artwork by Kate Kriege/© Gareth Stevens, Inc.; p. 18, © Sally Bensusen, 1988; p. 19 (inset), © Dudley Foster, Woods Hole Oceanographic Institution; pp. 20-21 (all), © Julian Baum, 1988; p. 22, photograph courtesy of NASA; p. 23 (both), © Imre Friedmann/copyright 1982 by the American Association for the Advancement of Science; p. 25 (both), © Doug McLeod, 1988; p. 27, © George Peirson, 1988; pp. 28-29 (house), artwork by Laurie Shock/© Gareth Stevens, Inc.; p. 28 (top), © J. Coggins, 1988; p. 28 (left center), © Theresa Fassel, 1988; p. 28 (bottom), © Marilyn Schaller, 1988; p. 29 (top left and bottom), © Runk/Schoenberger from Grant Heilman; p. 29 (upper right), © Betsy Esselman; p. 29 (upper center right), Science Photo Library; p. 29 (lower center right), © Marilyn Schaller.